Four

Ways to Be a Good Employee

Dedication

I want to always give the praise and glory to my Lord and Savior Jesus Christ. Never would have made it without you Lord, I love you so much.

To my Father, and Mother: Mom, Dad; I love you both very much, and I'm thankful you can see the Lord use your little son.

To Mychal, Randy, and Loretta: All three of us have taken paths in life, but one thing remains the same: I Love you, and look what the Lord is doing with your little brother.

To Stacey, Victoria and Kayla: You three are my inspiration, and thank God each and every day for blessing me to be your Father.

To my Pastor and Breakthrough family: God bless you and thank you for making feel at home.

Foreword

"A good man shows favor, and lends, he shall guide his affairs with discretion" (Scripture reference: Psalm 112:5, Kings James Version).

"See thou a man diligent in his business? He shall stand before kings; he shall not stand before mean men" (Scripture reference: Proverbs 22:29, Kings James Version).

I've been in the work force beginning at the age of 16 years old.

My first job was a messenger for the magazine "Redbook".

I transitioned from there to serving in our armed forces proudly for 11 years.

After leaving the United States Army, I worked as security officer at the John F. Kennedy Airport for eleven years.

In the years of employment, I've obtained, I've seen people come and go.

I've watched some excel in their field, while others took a more laid back attitude, and didn't take their job too seriously.

This attitude I remember came out so clearly September 11, 2001.

I was working as a ramp driver, when I heard the first of what sounded like thunder feel the air.

It was when I turned on the radio station, that I heard the announcement that a plane has struck the World Trade Center.

I watched in horror from my viewpoint from the airport, as the second plane hit the second Trade Center building.

The terror that filled the airport at the time was deafening.

I saw people scrambling to get as far away from the airport, in fear of another plane crashing into the area.

The security officers were told that no one could leave, until the area was deemed safe.

Some ignored that order, and left their assigned post, and one resigned that very day.

The comments I heard were "You're not paying me enough to stay here, and Whatever, I'll find another job somewhere else".

It shocked me, because during our training, it was emphasis, that in the case of a national emergency, all security officers are to remain on their post until further notice.

And, we all signed a form agreeing to this procedure.

In the years following that eventful day, I began to take notice of the level of commitment some had towards their job.

I thought about all the people, who were on the unemployment line looking for something to provide for their families, and the people who had a job, didn't seem to grasp that they were in a selective group of people, who at least were getting some sort of income coming into their house either weekly, or bi-weekly.

Through the years, and by personal observation, I learned that there are (4) essential ways to be classified as good employee.

Even-though, we should strive to be an employer, we have to remembered that everyone started as an employee first.

And because of certain traits, they moved from one position to another.

This is the purpose of this book.

To give you, what I believe is the keys to assist us in showing ourselves faithful over a few things, that we may be consider ruler of many.

"And if ye have not been faithful in that which is another man's, who shall give you that which is your own" (Scripture reference: Luke 16:12, Kings James Version).

Chapter I

Lesson#1-Be Grateful

"In everything give thanks, for this is the will of God, in Christ Jesus, concerning you" (Scripture reference: 1 Thessalonians 5:18, Kings James Version).

Every few months, the news media proudly displays the unemployment rate in America.

Every city unemployment is measure in this survey.

In NY city, for example to rate is 4.9%

While in California the rate is 5.6% percent.

The numbers are also broken into groups of people.

The unemployment rate among White-Americans is 4.6% percent.

While among African American is 9.0% percent.

You may ask: Why are showing these numbers, and what point are you trying to convey.

If you have a job, you're not part of this survey.

You're not among the people who are not working.

That's enough to Give God Praise for!! Out of the all the people who are searching the classified section of the newspapers every day, you can say: I HAVE A JOB.

Whether it's paying 8.00 or 15.00 an hour.

At the end of the week, you can be assured that you'll be getting some income into your bank account.

It may not be sufficient to pay all your bills, but with proper money management, and with Godly wisdom, every bill will be paid off.

That's why, you should come to your place of employment, thankful to have a place of employment.

Don't allow the attitude of others, determine the next eight hours of your day.

This is why, for the Child of God, before setting out towards work, we should spend quality time building up ourselves on our most holy faith (Scripture reference: Jude 1:20).

Praying for God's blessing to be upon us, that we when we walk into our work space, the peace of God will drive out any and all bad influence.

Believing God, that as our light so shine before men, as we work unto His Glory, it would be a testimony that will bring Praise and Honor to His name.

And, that someone will be drawn to us, and that would give us the opportunity to share the Gospel of Jesus Christ that can change anyone's life forever.

So, Be Grateful, Be Thankful, because there's someone else, who would love to have what you have. Always Give God the Highest Praise, for It Is he who gives you power to obtain wealth.

Chapter II

Lesson#2-Be Faithful.

"Moreover, it is required in stewards, that a man be found faithful". (Scripture reference: 1 Corinthians 4:2, Kings James Version).

At my Security Supervisor position at the J.F.K Airport, every six months we had an evaluation, and it was done by our manager.

One of the key points they emphasis was our attendance.

They considered one's commitment to arrive to work on time, was a sign of loyalty to the company.

It always surprised me, that there are a majority of workers who don't consider this an important issue.

They would arrive either five or ten minutes late, and thinking they have arrived at the appropriate time.

I remember, one employee would consistently come fifteen minutes late, and ask for a "leisure space", which means one cannot me consider late until after 15 minutes.

In the Word of God, Jacob was living in the land of Paddan Aram.

There was a man named Laban, he had two daughters: Rachel and Leah.

Jacob wanted to married Rachel, and he came to Laban asking for permission to marry his daughter.

Laban, made him work seven years in the field.

After the first seven years, He came to Laban, asking for his wife as payment for his faithfulness.

Laban, instead gave Jacob Leah as his wife, and made him work seven more years in the field.

Finally, after working in the field as required, Jacob and Rachel finally married.

The principle is this: Jacob remained faithful.

Working in the field is not easy.

It's gets hot, and windy, and sometime you may be required to work into the night.

But, he endured and was rewarded.

Even though, getting up early in the morning, and dealing with either traffic, or people on mass transit; faithfulness is always rewarded.

I, personally made it a point to arrive to work early, so my relief would know I was there, so they wouldn't have to worry about being relieved.

And your commitment to this principle, will be always be recognized by those in upper management.

Not only is faithfulness to arrive to work important, but adhering to the proper procedure is also critical.

I speak about my job at the airport in New York City, because of the high possibility of an attack that could take place.

We, were constantly on alert, and everyone was asked to perform their duties to the best of their ability.

There were many people who lost their positions, because of their lack of following the rules of the airport.

A soldier doesn't go from private to sergeant just because they show up for formation.

They are promoted, because of their desire to follow the instructions given to them by their subordinates.

The Apostle Paul, who wrote most of the New Testament, suffered many things for the cause of Christ.

He was shipwrecked, left on an island to die, bitten by a poisonous viper, and betrayed by own brothers in the ministry.

Not to mention, being constantly pursued by those oppose to the gospel of Jesus Christ.

But, at the end of His life this was his testimony: "I have fought a good faith, I have kept the faith".

Being Faithful to your place of employment is the key to Recognition and Promotion.

Chapter III

Lesson#3-Be Accountable.

"So then every one of us shall give an account of himself to God" (Scripture Reference: Romans 14:12, Kings James Version).

Accountable: (of a person, organization, or institution) required or expected to justify actions or decisions; responsible.

This is besides the previous ones we mentioned, an important lesson that will either make or break any employee.

Mistakes happens within an eight- hour period.

Things are not accomplished within the proper time, or not done within the proper guidelines.

When it does occur, someone has to be held accountable.

In the Word of God, in the book of Exodus, when Moses was on the mountain getting the ten commandments, Aaron his second in command, let the people persuade him to create a golden calf.

When Moses came down from the mountain, and saw what had taken place, he confronted Aaron, who blamed the people for what had happened.

And the same situation happened with King Saul.

He was commanded by the prophet Samuel to go into a certain land, and kill all the inhabitants.

Saul, kept some of people and cattle alive, and when Samuel asked him why he did not obey the commandment of God, he blamed the people.

I love it, when I watch the news, and some young person is arrested along with his friends, and each one blames the other for committing the crime.

This has happened many times in the work place.

And the true sign of maturity, is facing up when one makes a mistake.

In 1972, there was a break-in at the Watergate hotel.

The subsequent investigation uncovered a cover-up, that reached all the way to the White House, and it involved then President Richard Nixon.

Nixon, for many months denied any involvement in the cover-up, until it discovered that he was indeed involved.

This caused great distress in our nation, as we watched our leaders deceived many.

This is the result of not being accountable.

Owing up to one mistakes, is not a sign of weakness, but of growth.

Yes, there are consequences of making mistakes, but the greater mistake is trying to run from facing them.

An employee who admits when they are in error, is more likely to gain the respect of his peers, than one who doesn't admit their faults.

There's an old church hymn that's entitled: "It's me, It's me o Lord, standing in the need of prayer.

We, who are employees, must grasp that every actions we make outside the lines of the prescribed operational procedures, must be addressed by our subordinates.

Chapter IV

Lesson#4 Be Teachable

"Those things, which ye have both learned and received and heard, and seen in Me, do: and the God of peace shall be with you" (Scripture reference: Philippians 4:9, Kings James Version).

The final principle we will discuss is being teachable.

I've learned this, listening to many of my mentors:

"Parasites want what you have earned.

"Protégés want what you have learned.

Everyone wants to be the manager, the person in charge, the one who gives the order, and demands respect.

Very few, wants to be sat down, and taught the lessons one learned on their way to the top.

I've seen many come to into a job with zeal and enthusiasm, with a desire to move up in the company.

But, they refused to take wise counsel from others, thinking they need no teacher, that their zeal is the catalyst they need to succeed.

Sadly, they fizzle quickly.

I've been blessed with several mentors that has helped me in reaching my fullest potential.

Even, the disciples need a mentor named Jesus, to helped them in preparation for spreading the gospel.

Being teachable is a sign of humility, and that it will helped in business, and in life.

Bill Gates learned from his father.

Donald Trump (yes, that guy) inherited his business from his father.

Barbara Cochran, a mother of two, who had 20 other jobs, learned real estate from others, started her own company with $1,000, and has made doubled on the investment.

She credited all her success on her ability to listen, and be taught by others in her field.

Any employee desiring to go from where they are, to where they want to be, must be willing to take instruction, correction, and learn the wisdom and perseverance it took from others to succeed.

We spoke on the (4) Keys, I believe will help anyone be a good employee.

And when those in upper management, see an employee who follows these steps faithfully, they will be the one who will most likely be recognized and promoted.

And, I leave you with this: ALL THINGS ARE POSSIBLE TO HIM THAT BELIEVES!!!

Don't just be an employee, be the best, do your best, and watch promotion come your way.

Prayer

Father, I thank you again for allowing me to share these truths with my brother and sister.

I thank you Lord, you desire to bless us beyond what we can even ask, or imagine.

Thank you Lord for your precious Word, and I pray for the one who will read this book, that they use it and act on it, and believe you for the best in their lives in every area.

I pray, your favor, blessing and increase be upon them all in Jesus name

Amen!!

Prayer of Salvation

Perhaps, you are reading this book, and you don't have a personal relationship with the Lord Jesus Christ. You can have that today. Pray this simple prayer with me:

"Lord Jesus, come into my heart. Be my Savior and Lord". "Forgive me for all of my sins, cleanse me from all unrighteousness".

"I confess Jesus Christ as my Lord and Savior, and I believe God has raised Jesus from the dead just for me" (Scripture reference: Romans 10:9-10).

"And right now, I'm saved, healed, forgiven, and delivered". "I am a child of God, thank you Lord for saving me today".

If you prayed that prayer, please let us know. Send us an email at: markworship2003@yahoo.com.

God Bless You and Welcome to the Family!!!

LABLELED BUT
STILL USEFUL

MARK DUDLEY

Dream Fulfillment

Mark Dudley

These and all my books can be purchased at amazon.com and create space.com.